WITHDRAWN

3/06   27

WELCOME TO THE U.S.A.

WASHINGTON, D.C.

Written by Ann Heinrichs   Illustrated by Matt Kania
Content Adviser: Ryan Shepard, Collections Librarian,
City Museum of Washington, D.C., Washington, D.C.

The Child's World

Published in the United States of America by The Child's World®
PO Box 326 • Chanhassen, MN 55317-0326
800-599-READ • www.childsworld.com

Photo Credits
Cover: Photodisc; frontispiece: Medioimages.

Interior: Bill Falls: 34; Getty Images: 18 (Alex Wong), 25 (Hulton|Archive), 33 (Newsmakers); JackMcGuire.com/Washington, DC Convention & Tourism Corporation: 30, 38; Kelly-Mooney Photography/Corbis: 6, 9, 22; Photodisc: 21; Picture Desk/Travelsite/Global: 26; Carolyn Russo/National Air and Space Museum, Smithsonian Institution: 29; Washington, DC Convention & Tourism Corporation: 10, 14, 17; Tim Wright/Corbis: 13.

Acknowledgments
The Child's World®: Mary Berendes, Publishing Director

Editorial Directions, Inc.: E. Russell Primm, Editorial Director; Katie Marsico, Associate Editor; Judith Shiffer, Assistant Editor; Matt Messbarger, Editorial Assistant; Susan Hindman, Copy Editor; Melissa McDaniel, Proofreader; Kevin Cunningham, Peter Garnham, Matt Messbarger, Olivia Nellums, Chris Simms, Molly Symmonds, Katherine Trickle, Carl Stephen Wender, Fact Checkers; Tim Griffin/IndexServ, Indexer; Cian Loughlin O'Day, Photo Researcher and Editor

The Design Lab: Kathleen Petelinsek, Design; Julia Goozen, Art Production

Library of Congress Cataloging-in-Publication Data
Heinrichs, Ann.
   Washington, D.C. / by Ann Heinrichs ; cartography and illustrations by Matt Kania.
      p. cm. — (Welcome to the U.S.A.)
   Includes index.
   ISBN 1-59296-492-3 (library bound : alk. paper) 1. Washington (D.C.)—Juvenile literature. I. Kania, Matt, ill. II. Title.
   F194.3.H453 2006
   975.3—dc22   2005008822

Ann Heinrichs is the author of more than 100 books for children and young adults. She has also enjoyed successful careers as a children's book editor and an advertising copywriter. Ann grew up in Fort Smith, Arkansas, and lives in Chicago, Illinois.

About the Author
Ann Heinrichs

Matt Kania loves maps and, as a kid, dreamed of making them. In school he studied geography and cartography, and today he makes maps for a living. Matt's favorite thing about drawing maps is learning about the places they represent. Many of the maps he has created can be found in books, magazines, videos, Web sites, and public places.

About the
Map Illustrator
Matt Kania

On the cover: Wow! There must be a lot of important people in the Capitol!
On page one: The Lincoln Memorial makes everyone feel small!

OUR WASHINGTON, D.C., TRIP

Washington, D.C.'s Nicknames:
The Nation's Capital and the Capital City

Ready for a tour of our nation's capital? That's Washington, D.C.! It's full of places to explore.

You'll visit the president's house. You'll learn where the lawmakers meet. You'll see fireworks and cherry blossoms. You'll ride boats and wander through woods. You'll gaze up at dinosaurs and spaceships. And you'll watch millions of dollars being printed!

Don't wait. Just follow that loopy dotted line. Or skip around to make your own tour. Now, buckle up and hang on tight. We're off to see the capital!

WELCOME TO WASHINGTON, D.C.

As you travel through Washington, D.C., watch for all the interesting facts along the way.

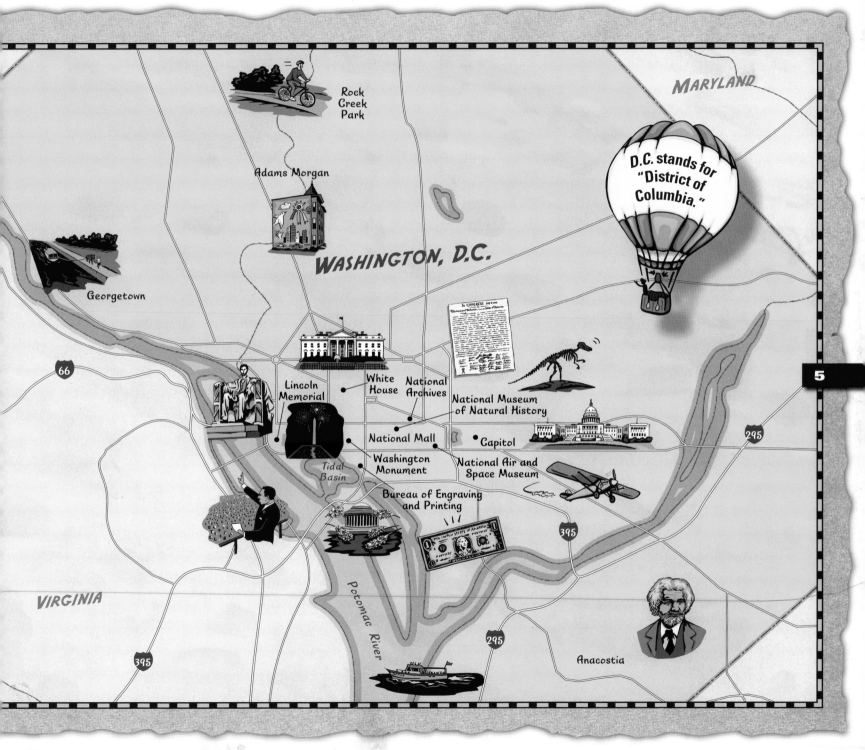

MARYLAND

Rock Creek Park

Adams Morgan

WASHINGTON, D.C.

Georgetown

D.C. stands for "District of Columbia."

Lincoln Memorial

White House

National Archives

National Museum of Natural History

National Mall

Capitol

National Air and Space Museum

Washington Monument

Tidal Basin

Bureau of Engraving and Printing

VIRGINIA

Potomac River

Anacostia

66

295

395

295

395

6

Boating along the Potomac

Would you like to see Washington, D.C.'s sights? Just ride a boat on the Potomac River!

The Potomac River flows alongside Washington, D.C. It forms the city's southwest border. Across the river is the state of Virginia. Maryland surrounds the city's other sides.

Washington is divided into four **quadrants.** They're called northwest, northeast, southeast, and southwest. For short, they're called N.W., N.E., S.E., and S.W. Every address carries one of these abbreviations. There are north-south, east-west, and **diagonal** streets. Many streets meet in squares or circles.

What a view! Visitors enjoy a sunset cruise on the Potomac River.

The Anacostia River branches off from the Potomac River. It flows through eastern Washington, D.C.

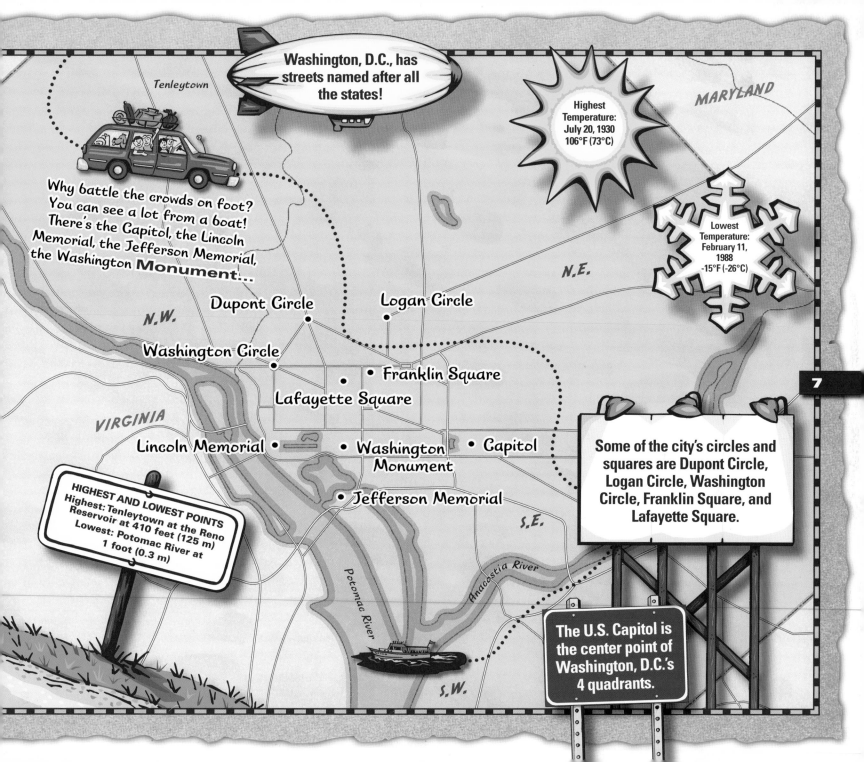

Washington, D.C., has streets named after all the states!

Tenleytown

Why battle the crowds on foot? You can see a lot from a boat! There's the Capitol, the Lincoln Memorial, the Jefferson Memorial, the Washington **Monument**...

MARYLAND

Highest Temperature: July 20, 1930 106°F (73°C)

Lowest Temperature: February 11, 1988 -15°F (-26°C)

N.E.

N.W.

Dupont Circle

Logan Circle

Washington Circle

Franklin Square

Lafayette Square

VIRGINIA

Lincoln Memorial

Washington Monument

Capitol

Jefferson Memorial

HIGHEST AND LOWEST POINTS
Highest: Tenleytown at the Reno Reservoir at 410 feet (125 m)
Lowest: Potomac River at 1 foot (0.3 m)

S.E.

Some of the city's circles and squares are Dupont Circle, Logan Circle, Washington Circle, Franklin Square, and Lafayette Square.

Potomac River

Anacostia River

S.W.

The U.S. Capitol is the center point of Washington, D.C.'s 4 quadrants.

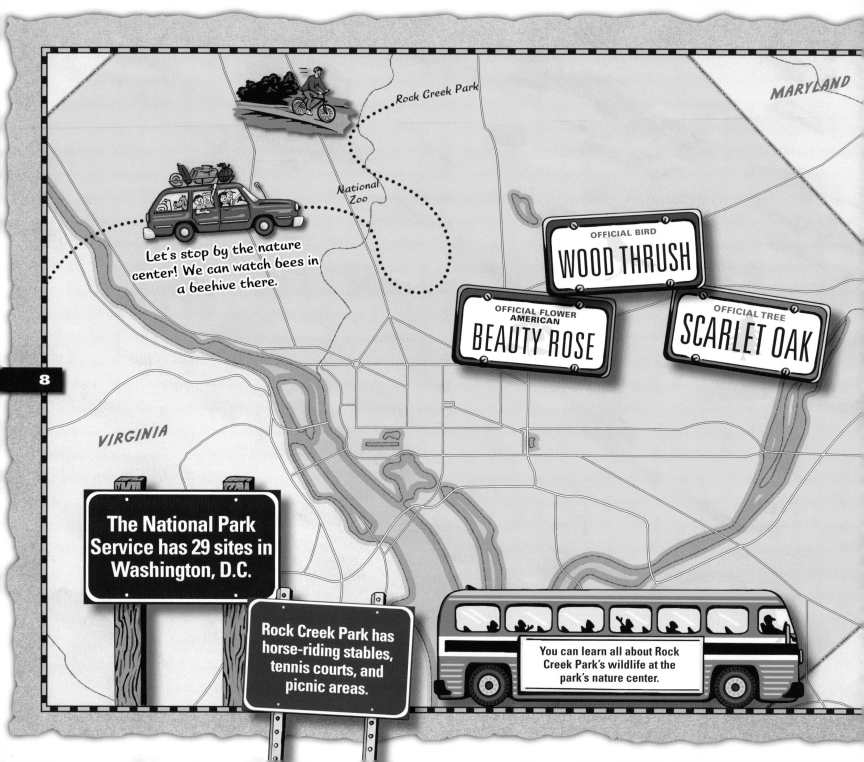

MARYLAND

Rock Creek Park

National Zoo

Let's stop by the nature center! We can watch bees in a beehive there.

OFFICIAL BIRD
WOOD THRUSH

OFFICIAL FLOWER
AMERICAN
BEAUTY ROSE

OFFICIAL TREE
SCARLET OAK

VIRGINIA

The National Park Service has 29 sites in Washington, D.C.

Rock Creek Park has horse-riding stables, tennis courts, and picnic areas.

You can learn all about Rock Creek Park's wildlife at the park's nature center.

Exploring Rock Creek Park

Wander through Rock Creek Park. Thick woods are all around you. A stone bridge crosses the creek. You may see foxes, rabbits, squirrels, and deer. It's hard to believe you're inside a city!

Washington, D.C., has hundreds of parks. Some have statues, benches, and flowerbeds. Others are almost like big forests.

Rock Creek Park is the city's biggest park. It's in the northwest part of town. Bike paths and nature trails wind through the park. You can play soccer or tennis there. And you can have picnics, too!

Giddy up! Visitors can explore Rock Creek Park on horseback.

The National Zoo is in Rock Creek Park. The zoo is home to more than 2,700 animals.

The Chesapeake and Ohio Canal operated from 1850 to 1924.

Don't want to take a boat tour? Simply stroll alongside the Chesapeake and Ohio Canal.

Many historians think Georgetown was named after King George II of England.

Riding the Chesapeake and Ohio Canal

Head on over to the Georgetown neighborhood. Then hop aboard the canal boat. You'll ride past old storage buildings. And a mule pulls your boat along!

You're riding on the Chesapeake and Ohio Canal. It runs beside the Potomac River. Native Americans once fished in this river. English settlers arrived in the 1600s. They began growing tobacco.

Georgetown was founded in 1751. It became an important tobacco trading center. Planters stored and sold tobacco there. Tons of tobacco were shipped from Georgetown's port. The canal was built in the 1800s. It mostly carried coal to **inland** towns.

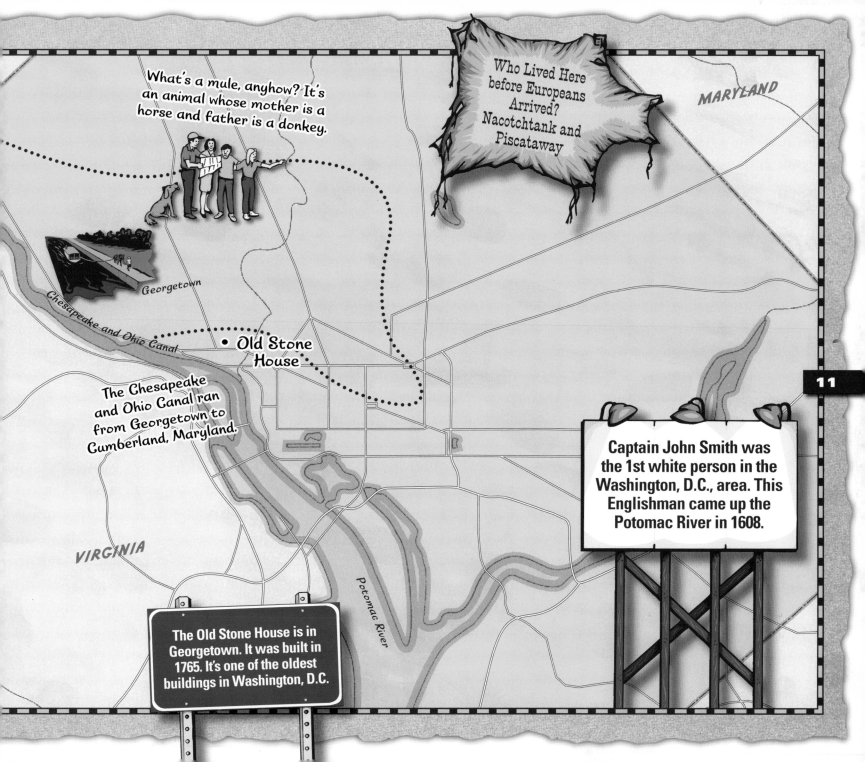

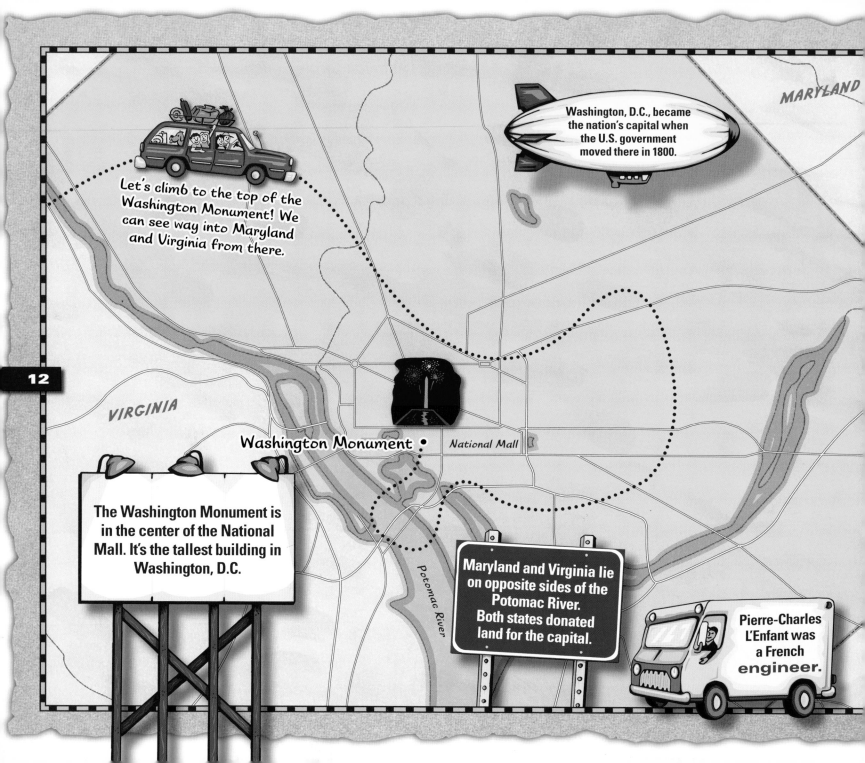

Fireworks over the Washington Monument

The fireworks explode in brilliant colors. They light up the tall, white tower. It's the Fourth of July on the National Mall!

The National Mall is a long, tree-lined park. It's the center of activity in Washington, D.C. That white tower is the Washington Monument. It honors George Washington, our first president.

Washington decided to build the capital city here. He chose the spot in 1791. Washington asked Pierre-Charles L'Enfant to design the city. L'Enfant's plan called for wide streets. He also included land for parks and monuments.

Hooray for the red, white, and blue! Fireworks explode over the Washington Monument on Independence Day.

New York City was the nation's capital from 1785 to 1790. Then the capital moved to Philadelphia, Pennsylvania.

The Capitol has 540 rooms on 5 floors!

The Capitol

National lawmakers are hard at work inside the Capitol.

The U.S. Congress has 2 sections. They are the Senate and the House of Representatives.

Face east as you walk along the Mall. You see a big white building. It stands high on Capitol Hill. It's the U.S. Capitol!

This building is where the U.S. Congress meets. Members of Congress are the nation's lawmakers. They come from every part of the country.

Our national government is split into three branches. The lawmakers make up one branch. Another branch carries out the laws. The U.S. president heads this branch. The third branch is made up of judges. They decide whether someone has broken a law.

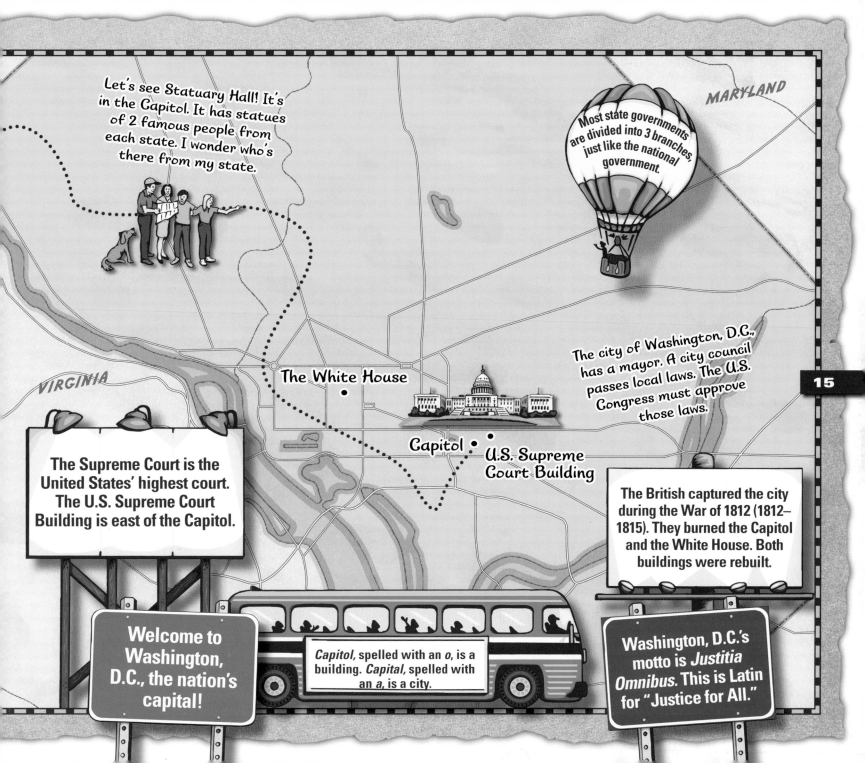

Let's see Statuary Hall! It's in the Capitol. It has statues of 2 famous people from each state. I wonder who's there from my state.

Most state governments are divided into 3 branches, just like the national government.

MARYLAND

The city of Washington, D.C., has a mayor. A city council passes local laws. The U.S. Congress must approve those laws.

VIRGINIA

The White House

Capitol

U.S. Supreme Court Building

The Supreme Court is the United States' highest court. The U.S. Supreme Court Building is east of the Capitol.

The British captured the city during the War of 1812 (1812–1815). They burned the Capitol and the White House. Both buildings were rebuilt.

Welcome to Washington, D.C., the nation's capital!

Capitol, spelled with an *o,* is a building. *Capital,* spelled with an *a,* is a city.

Washington, D.C.'s motto is *Justitia Omnibus.* This is Latin for "Justice for All."

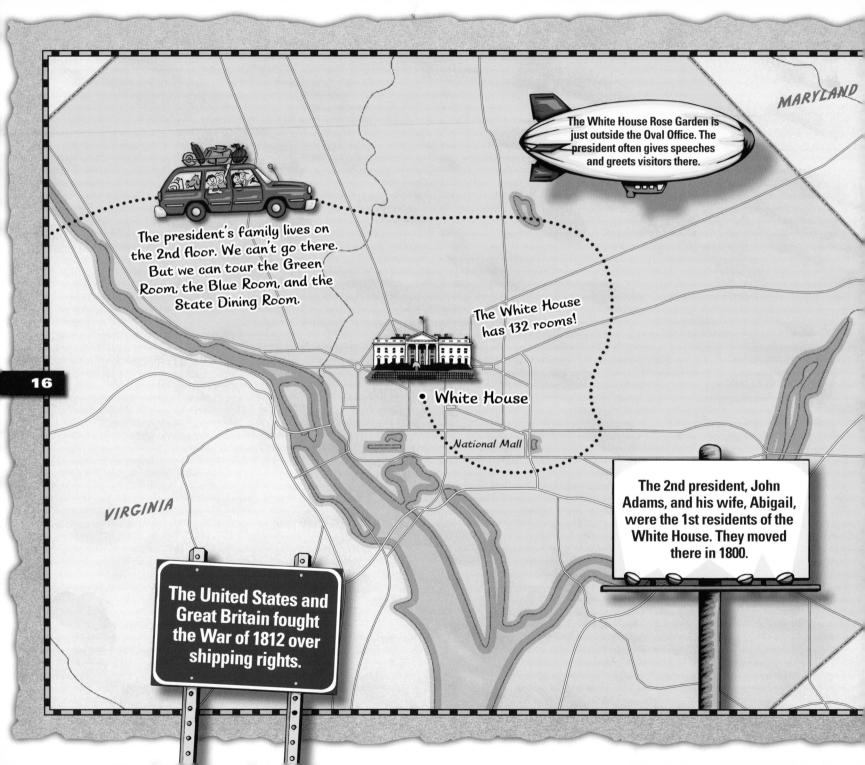

The White House Rose Garden is just outside the Oval Office. The president often gives speeches and greets visitors there.

The president's family lives on the 2nd floor. We can't go there. But we can tour the Green Room, the Blue Room, and the State Dining Room.

The White House has 132 rooms!

White House

National Mall

The 2nd president, John Adams, and his wife, Abigail, were the 1st residents of the White House. They moved there in 1800.

MARYLAND

VIRGINIA

The United States and Great Britain fought the War of 1812 over shipping rights.

The White House

It's white. And it's a house. What can it be? It's the White House, of course! That's where the president's offices are. The president's family lives there, too. It's just north of the National Mall.

Several hundred people work at the White House. Some help the president with national business. Others take care of household jobs. Guards, maids, and chefs all work there.

Government workers are everywhere in Washington, D.C. Government is the city's biggest **industry.** Tourism is an important industry, too. Millions of people visit the capital every year.

Can your front yard compare to this? Monuments decorate the lawn of the White House.

The president's main office in the White House is called the Oval Office.

Guards watch over precious documents at the National Archives.

The National Archives

Billions of documents are in the National Archives. This building holds the nation's official papers. But most visitors look for three special documents.

One is the Declaration of Independence. It was signed on July 4, 1776. **Colonists** were declaring freedom from Great Britain.

Another treasure is the U.S. Constitution. It outlines the nation's basic laws. The third document is the Bill of Rights. It promises basic rights and freedoms to all. That includes freedom of speech.

All three documents are very old originals. They're safely displayed in glass cases. They show what the United States is all about!

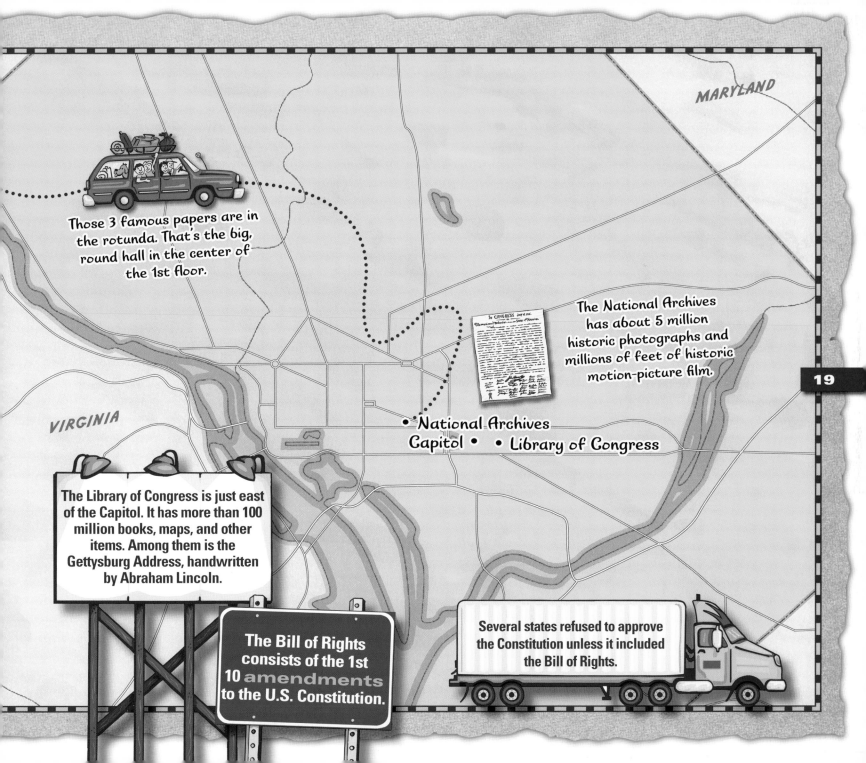

Those 3 famous papers are in the rotunda. That's the big, round hall in the center of the 1st floor.

The National Archives has about 5 million historic photographs and millions of feet of historic motion-picture film.

MARYLAND

VIRGINIA

• National Archives
Capitol •   • Library of Congress

The Library of Congress is just east of the Capitol. It has more than 100 million books, maps, and other items. Among them is the Gettysburg Address, handwritten by Abraham Lincoln.

The Bill of Rights consists of the 1st 10 amendments to the U.S. Constitution.

Several states refused to approve the Constitution unless it included the Bill of Rights.

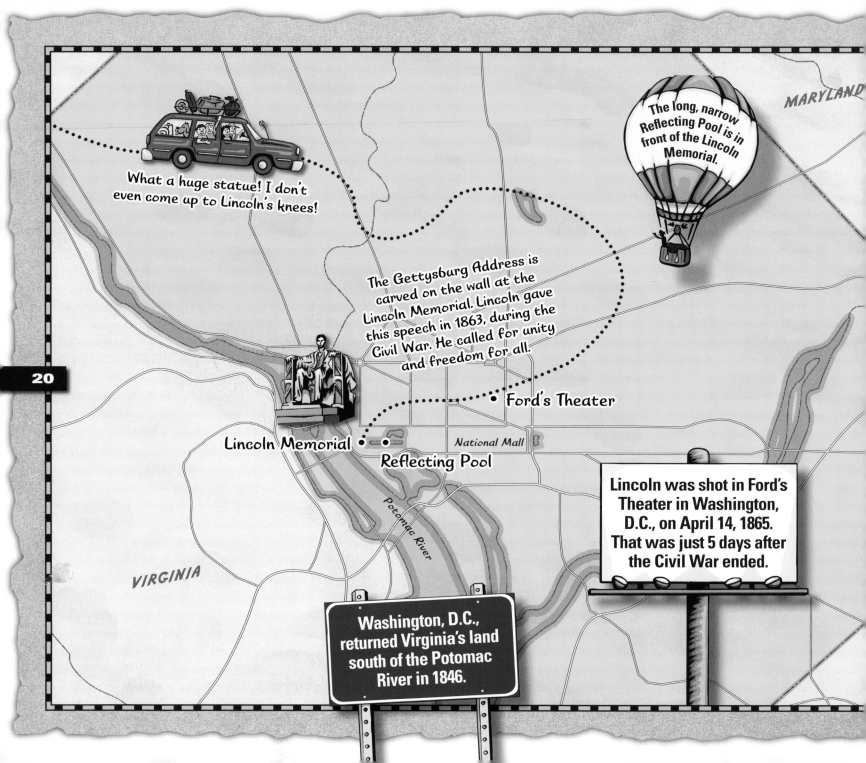

The Lincoln Memorial and the Civil War

The giant statue sits in a giant chair. He seems to gaze out over the Mall. It's Abraham Lincoln, the sixteenth president. He has his own monument—the Lincoln Memorial!

Lincoln was president during the Civil War (1861–1865). Northern and Southern states fought this war over slavery. The Northern, or Union, side opposed slavery. Southern, or Confederate, states wanted to keep slavery. Lincoln worked hard to keep the nation together. In the end, the Union won. Then all the slaves were freed.

Sadly, Lincoln had many enemies. He was shot and killed in 1865. But he's still a symbol of freedom for all.

Want to learn about our 16th president? Just head to the Lincoln Memorial.

Construction began on the Lincoln Memorial on February 12, 1914. That was Lincoln's 105th birthday!

Are you back in the 1800s? No, you're just touring the home of Frederick Douglass!

Anacostia began as Uniontown in 1854. It was a community for people who worked at Washington's navy yard.

Frederick Douglass's Home in Anacostia

Frederick Douglass was a slave, but he escaped. Then he worked hard to end slavery. He wrote articles and gave speeches for years. Now you can visit Frederick Douglass's home. It's in the Anacostia neighborhood. Douglass lived there from 1877 to 1895.

Anacostia is one of the capital's many neighborhoods. Most of its residents are African American.

Washington, D.C., was really crowded by 1950. The government began opening offices in the **suburbs.** Government workers had been moving out for years, too. Today, thousands of government workers live outside Washington, D.C. They have homes nearby in Maryland or Virginia.

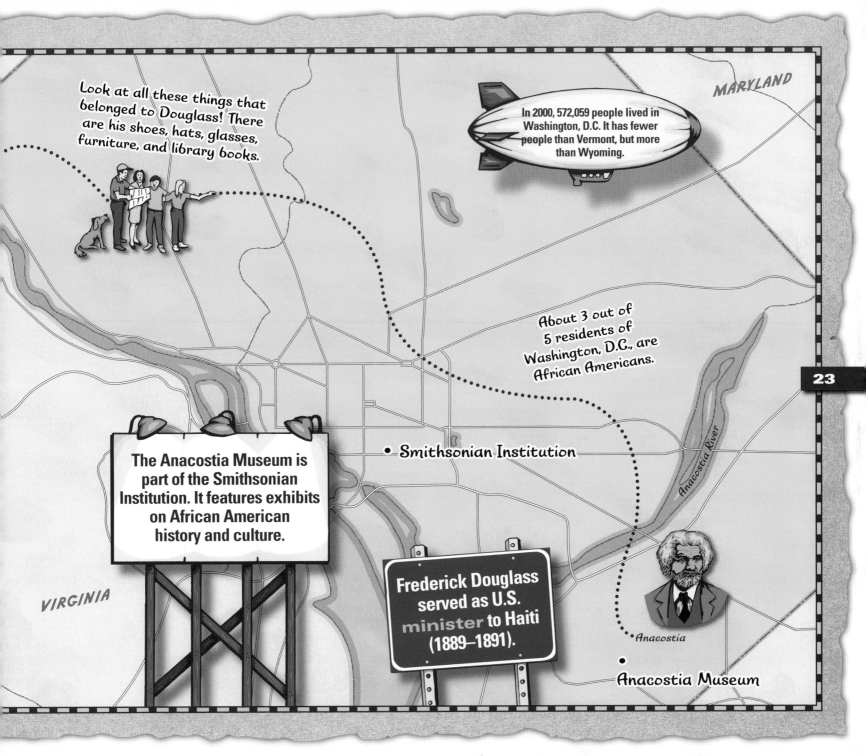

Look at all these things that belonged to Douglass! There are his shoes, hats, glasses, furniture, and library books.

In 2000, 572,059 people lived in Washington, D.C. It has fewer people than Vermont, but more than Wyoming.

MARYLAND

About 3 out of 5 residents of Washington, D.C., are African Americans.

Smithsonian Institution

The Anacostia Museum is part of the Smithsonian Institution. It features exhibits on African American history and culture.

Frederick Douglass served as U.S. minister to Haiti (1889–1891).

Anacostia River

VIRGINIA

Anacostia

Anacostia Museum

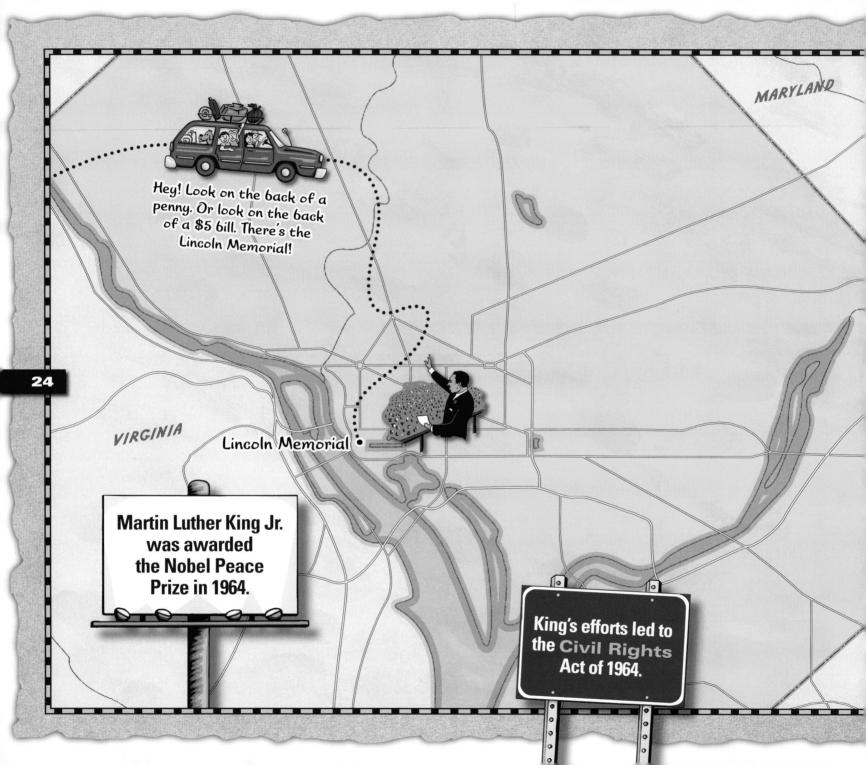

Gatherings at the Lincoln Memorial

Stand on the steps of the Lincoln Memorial. Look out and imagine huge crowds. Many crowds have gathered here over the years. They come to show unity in their beliefs.

Dr. Martin Luther King Jr. stood here in 1963. He worked for equal rights for African Americans. About 250,000 people came to hear him speak.

"I have a dream," said King. He dreamed that everyone could live as equals. He dreamed that they could live in friendship. He imagined all people joining hands and singing, "We are free at last!" King's words were deeply moving. People still remember them today.

King made his famous speech in 1963.
He was killed in 1968.

King delivered his "I have a dream" speech on August 28, 1963.

Is this the circus? Nope—it's the National Museum of Natural History!

The Kennedy Center's full name is the John F. Kennedy Center for the Performing Arts. It's on the bank of the Potomac River in the Foggy Bottom neighborhood.

The National Museum of Natural History

The *Allosaurus* is ready to strike. The *Tyrannosaurus* is ready to bite. Help!

Don't run off just yet. You're safe from attack. You're visiting the National Museum of Natural History! Its dinosaur hall is packed with frightful creatures.

Many museums line the National Mall. One is the National Museum of Natural History. It's part of the Smithsonian Institution.

Visitors love Washington, D.C.'s museums. They enjoy shows at the Kennedy Center, too. Are you a sports fan? There's plenty for you to see. The city has several great teams you can watch.

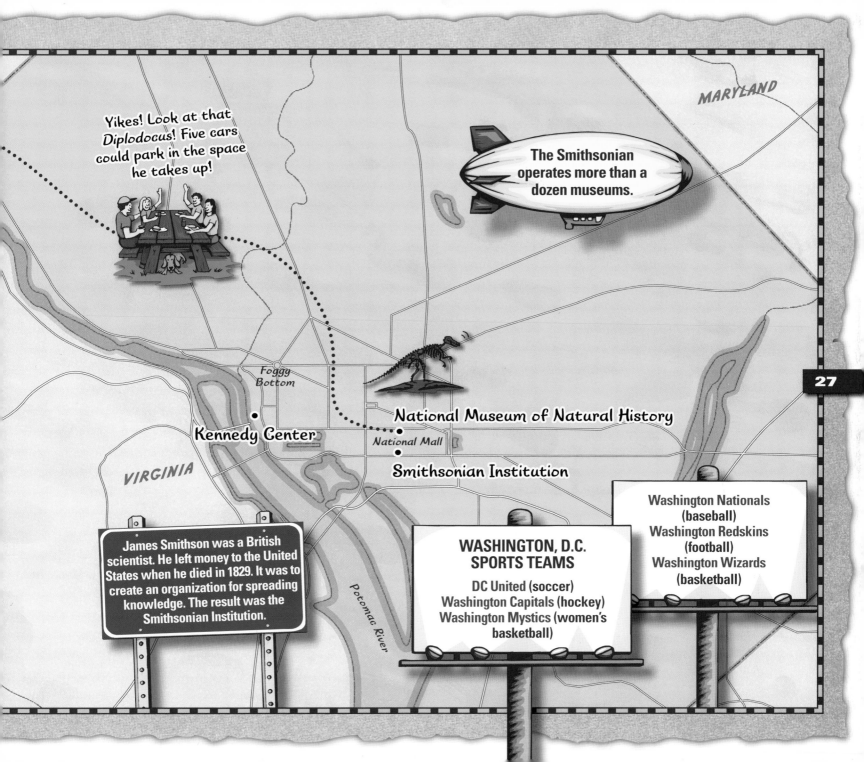

Yikes! Look at that *Diplodocus*! Five cars could park in the space he takes up!

The Smithsonian operates more than a dozen museums.

MARYLAND

Foggy Bottom

National Museum of Natural History

Kennedy Center

National Mall

Smithsonian Institution

VIRGINIA

James Smithson was a British scientist. He left money to the United States when he died in 1829. It was to create an organization for spreading knowledge. The result was the Smithsonian Institution.

WASHINGTON, D.C. SPORTS TEAMS

**DC United (soccer)
Washington Capitals (hockey)
Washington Mystics (women's basketball)**

**Washington Nationals (baseball)
Washington Redskins (football)
Washington Wizards (basketball)**

Potomac River

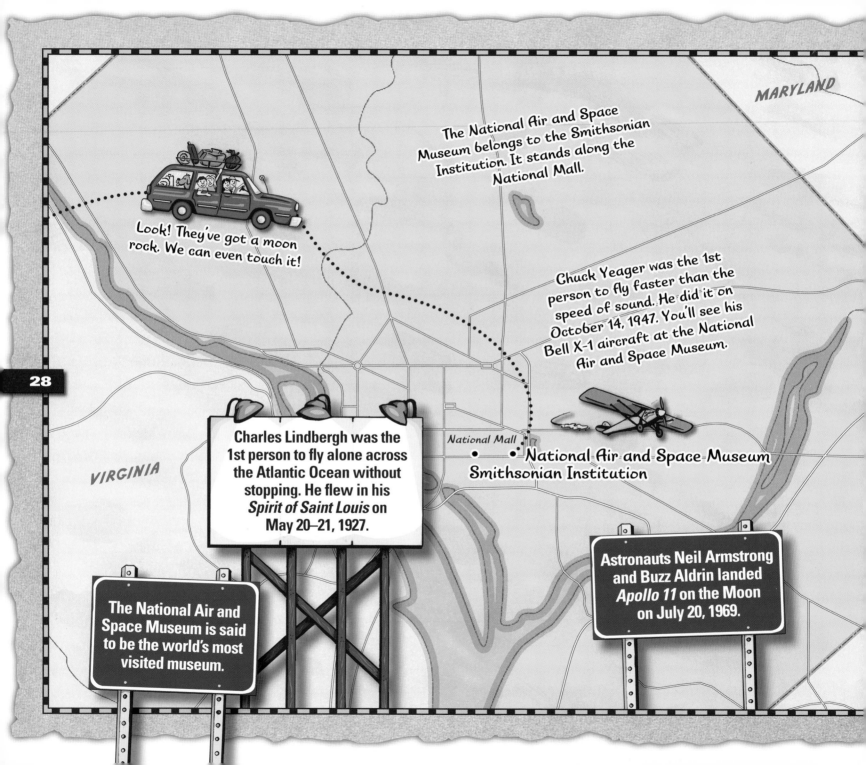

The National Air and Space Museum

Orville and Wilbur Wright made their 1st flight on December 17, 1903.

Do you dream of flying and exploring space? You're not alone. The mysteries of flight have always excited humans. Just visit the National Air and Space Museum. You'll learn how dreams of flight became real!

You'll see the Wright brothers' 1903 plane. They invented the first power-driven aircraft. You'll see the *Spirit of Saint Louis*. It flew across the Atlantic Ocean in 1927. And you'll gaze at *Apollo 11*. It took the first U.S. astronauts to the Moon!

If you visit, get there early. More than nine million people visit every year!

Would you make a good pilot? Find out at the National Air and Space Museum.

29

Cherry Blossom Time

Is it springtime? Then it's cherry blossom time!

About 3,750 cherry trees grow near the Potomac. The best-known trees surround the Tidal Basin. That's a pond just south of the Mall. The first trees were planted in 1912. They were gifts from the people of Japan.

The pink and white flowers are awesome. When's the best time to see them? During the Cherry Blossom Festival! It's held in late March and early April. It attracts thousands of people from around the world.

Spring is in the air! Cherry trees blossom near the Jefferson Memorial.

The National Arboretum is a huge park in northeast Washington. It displays thousands of trees and shrubs.

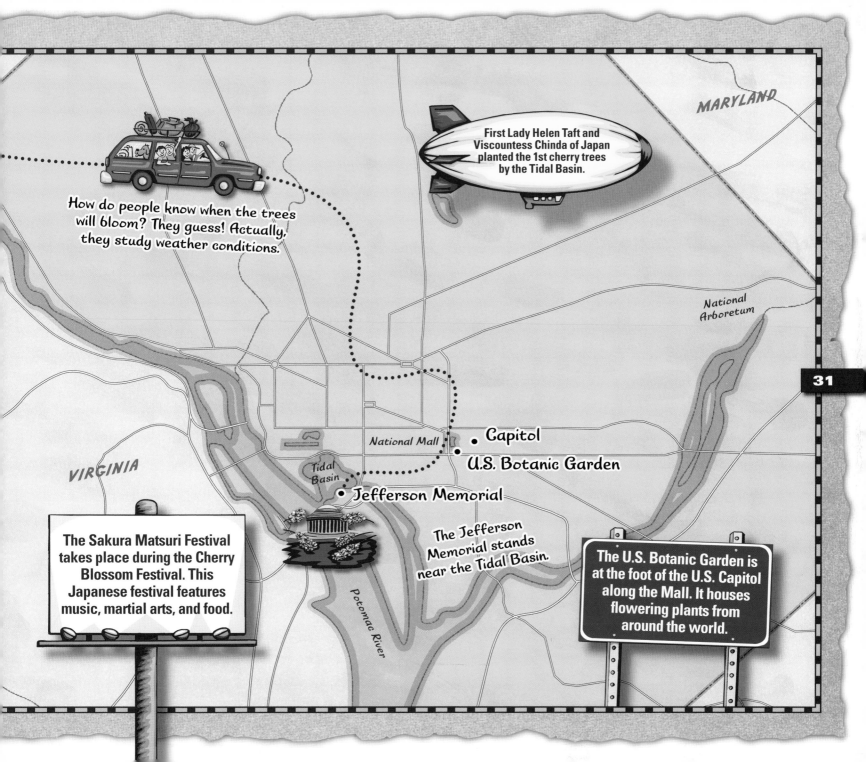

How do people know when the trees will bloom? They guess! Actually, they study weather conditions.

First Lady Helen Taft and Viscountess Chinda of Japan planted the 1st cherry trees by the Tidal Basin.

MARYLAND

National Arboretum

• Capitol

National Mall

U.S. Botanic Garden

VIRGINIA

Tidal Basin

• Jefferson Memorial

The Jefferson Memorial stands near the Tidal Basin.

The Sakura Matsuri Festival takes place during the Cherry Blossom Festival. This Japanese festival features music, martial arts, and food.

The U.S. Botanic Garden is at the foot of the U.S. Capitol along the Mall. It houses flowering plants from around the world.

Potomac River

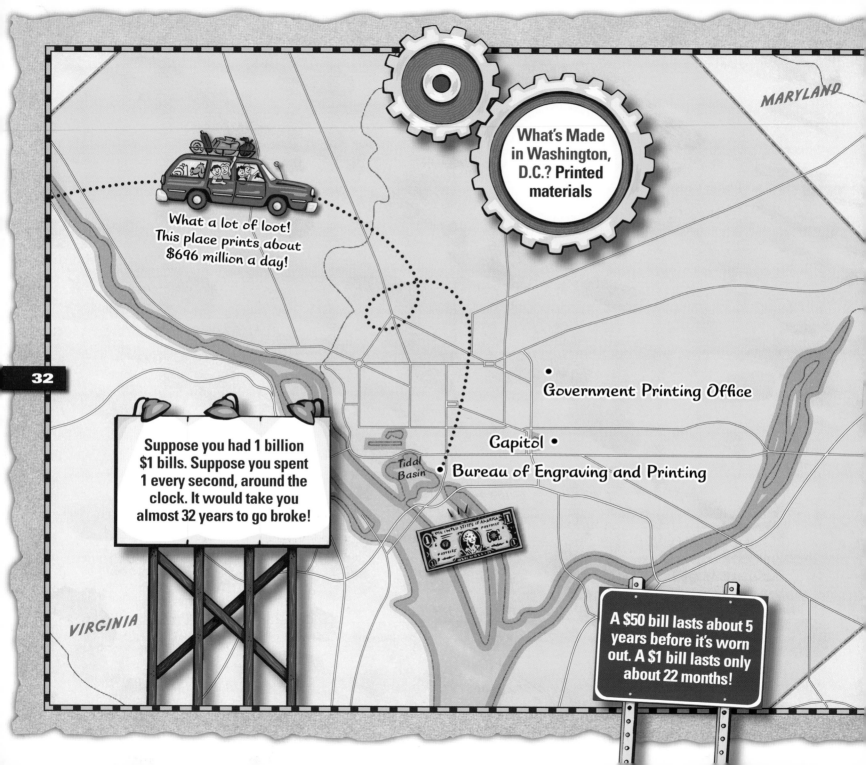

MARYLAND

What a lot of loot!
This place prints about
$696 million a day!

What's Made
in Washington,
D.C.? Printed
materials

Government Printing Office

Suppose you had 1 billion
$1 bills. Suppose you spent
1 every second, around the
clock. It would take you
almost 32 years to go broke!

Capitol

Tidal
Basin

Bureau of Engraving and Printing

VIRGINIA

A $50 bill lasts about 5
years before it's worn
out. A $1 bill lasts only
about 22 months!

The Bureau of Engraving and Printing

The printing presses buzz and whir. Big sheets of paper zoom through them. Then the paper is cut. What's the finished product? Money!

You're touring the Bureau of Engraving and Printing. It's just east of the Tidal Basin. It prints our paper money. You'll see millions of dollars there!

Washington, D.C., doesn't have many factories. The main factory activities are printing and publishing. Most printing is done for the government. Printing money is one example. Many government documents need to be printed, too. The Government Printing Office does this job.

Need some extra cash? Dollar bills are printed at the Bureau of Engraving and Printing.

The Government Printing Office is north of the Capitol. It prints documents for all 3 branches of government.

Do you like art? Check out the murals in Adams Morgan!

Adams Morgan can be found around 18th Street and Columbia Road.

Murals in Adams Morgan

Cruise through Adams Morgan. That's a neighborhood in northwest Washington, D.C. The area is home to many **Hispanic** people. You'll see huge, colorful murals, or wall paintings.

Some paintings show people working or playing. Others show animals or historic figures. Washington, D.C., has many other interesting neighborhoods. Many are named for the circles and squares they are by. Wealthy people first built up the area around Dupont Circle. Now the area has many **embassies** and museums.

The Lafayette Square neighborhood is near the White House. Georgetown is known for its shops and restaurants. The city has many more neighborhoods.

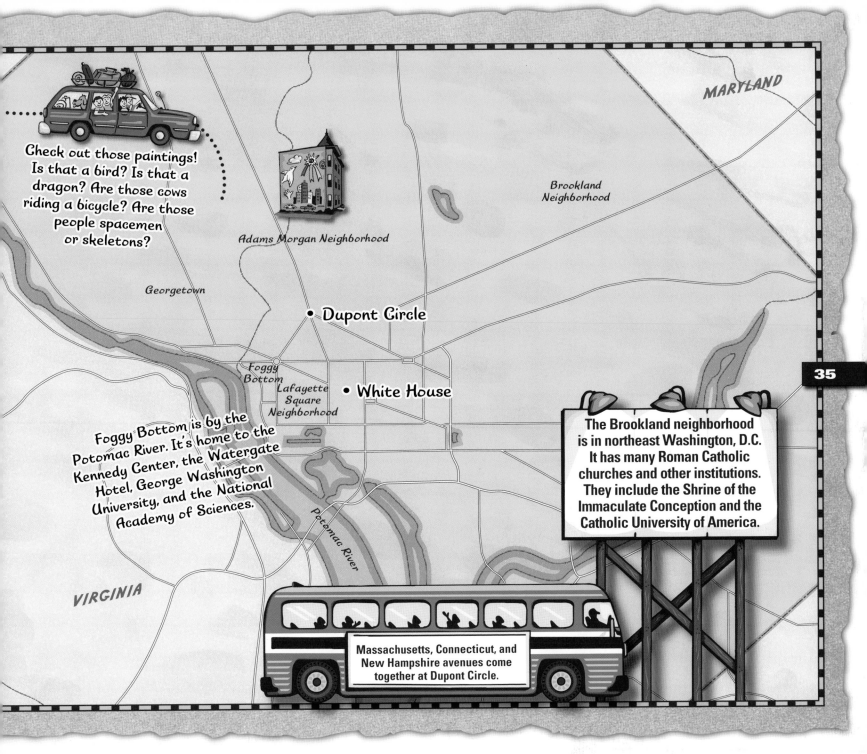

Check out those paintings! Is that a bird? Is that a dragon? Are those cows riding a bicycle? Are those people spacemen or skeletons?

MARYLAND

Brookland Neighborhood

Adams Morgan Neighborhood

Georgetown

• Dupont Circle

Foggy Bottom

Lafayette Square Neighborhood

• White House

Foggy Bottom is by the Potomac River. It's home to the Kennedy Center, the Watergate Hotel, George Washington University, and the National Academy of Sciences.

The Brookland neighborhood is in northeast Washington, D.C. It has many Roman Catholic churches and other institutions. They include the Shrine of the Immaculate Conception and the Catholic University of America.

Potomac River

VIRGINIA

Massachusetts, Connecticut, and New Hampshire avenues come together at Dupont Circle.

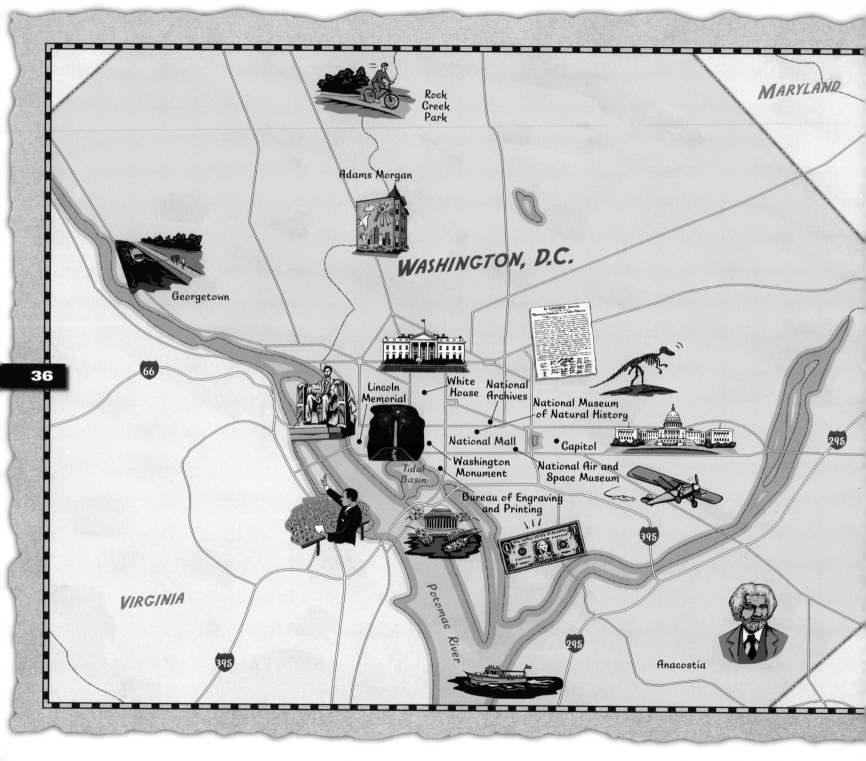

MARYLAND

Rock
Creek
Park

Adams Morgan

WASHINGTON, D.C.

Georgetown

66

Lincoln
Memorial

White
House

National
Archives

National Museum
of Natural History

National Mall

Capitol

295

Washington
Monument

National Air and
Space Museum

Tidal
Basin

Bureau of Engraving
and Printing

395

VIRGINIA

Potomac River

395

295

Anacostia

OUR TRIP

We visited many amazing places on our trip! We also met a lot of interesting people along the way. Look at the map on the left. Use your finger to trace all the places we have been.

How many animals live in the National Zoo? See page 9 for the answer.

Who was Georgetown possibly named after? Page 10 has the answer.

When was New York City the nation's capital? See page 13 for the answer.

What kinds of statues does Statuary Hall feature? Look on page 15 for the answer.

How many rooms are in the White House? Page 16 has the answer.

Where was Abraham Lincoln shot? Turn to page 20 for the answer.

What did Chuck Yeager do in 1947? Look on page 28 for the answer.

How long does a $50 bill last before it wears out? Turn to page 32 for the answer.

That was a great trip! We have traveled all over Washington, D.C.!

There are a few places that we didn't have time for, though. Next time, we plan to visit the Capital Children's Museum on Capitol Hill. Visitors can learn about various cultures and tour a prehistoric cave! They can also watch scientific experiments and even perform some of their own.

More Places to Visit in Washington, D.C.

WORDS TO KNOW

amendments (uh-MEND-muhnts) changes or additions

civil rights (SIV-il RITES) the rights of a citizen

colonists (KOL-uh-nists) people who settle a new land for their home country

diagonal (dye-AG-uh-nuhl) a slanted angle

embassies (EM-buh-seez) offices of representatives of foreign countries

engineer (en-juh-NIHR) someone who designs or builds machines, vehicles, bridges, roads, or other structures

Hispanic (hiss-PAN-ik) coming from or having to do with countries where Spanish is spoken

industry (IN-duh-stree) a type of business

inland (IN-luhnd) away from coastal areas

minister (MIN-uh-stur) a representative of a foreign country

monument (MON-yuh-muhnt) a large marker that honors a person or event

quadrants (KWAH-druhnts) sections created by cutting a circle into 4 equal parts

suburbs (SUHB-urbz) communities at the edge or just outside of a large city

Washington, D.C., covers 61 square miles (158 sq km). It's smaller in size than any state.

OFFICIAL SYMBOLS

Bird: Wood thrush

Flower: American beauty rose

Tree: Scarlet oak

Official flag

Official seal

OFFICIAL SONG

"Washington"

Words and music by Jimmie Dodd

Washington, the fairest city in the greatest land of all,
Named for one, our country's father who first answered freedom's call,
God bless our White House, our Capitol too,
and keep ever flying the Red, White and Blue,

Grandest spot beneath the sun is Washington.

Oh the cherry blossoms bring a lot of joy each Spring,
and the statue of Abe Lincoln greets your eye,
When parades pass in review down Pennsylvania Avenue,
ev'rybody lifts their voices to the sky!

Washington, the fairest city in the greatest land of all,
Named for one, our country's father who first answered freedom's call,
God bless our White House, our Capitol too,
and keep ever flying the Red, White and Blue,
Grandest spot beneath the sun is Washington.

FAMOUS PEOPLE

Albee, Edward (1928–), playwright

Bernstein, Carl (1944–), journalist

Chappelle, David (1973–), comedian and actor

Chasez, J. C. (1976–), singer

Chung, Connie (1946–), television newscaster

Danziger, Paula (1944–2004), children's author

Davis, Benjamin Oliver, Jr. (1912–2002), leader of the Tuskegee Airmen

Davis, Benjamin Oliver, Sr. (1877–1970), 1st African American general

Dulles, John Foster (1888–1959), lawyer and diplomat

Ellington, Duke (1899–1974), jazz musician

Gaye, Marvin (1939–1984), singer and songwriter

Gore, Al (1948–), politician

Hawn, Goldie (1945–), actor

Hoover, J. Edgar (1895–1972), 1st director of the FBI

Hurt, William (1950–), actor

Jackson, Samuel L. (1948–), actor

Kennedy, John Fitzgerald, Jr. (1960–1999), lawyer and publisher

Leonard, Sugar Ray (1956–), boxer

Sousa, John Philip (1854–1932), composer

Williams, Anthony (1951–), politician

TO FIND OUT MORE

At the Library
Benson, Laura Lee, and Iris Van Rynbach (illustrator). *Washington, D.C.: A Scrapbook.* Watertown, Mass.: Charlesbridge, 1999.

Gilmore, Frederic. *The Lincoln Memorial: A Great President Remembered.* Chanhassen, Minn.: The Child's World, 2001.

Gilmore, Frederic. *The Washington Monument: A Tribute to a Man, a Monument for a Nation.* Chanhassen, Minn.: The Child's World, 2001.

Karr, Kathleen, and Paul Meisel (illustrator). *It Happened in the White House: Extraordinary Tales from America's Most Famous Home.* New York: Hyperion Books for Children, 2000.

On the Web
Visit our home page for lots of links about Washington, D.C.:
http://www.childsworld.com/links

Note to Parents, Teachers, and Librarians: We routinely verify our Web links to make sure they are safe, active sites—so encourage your readers to check them out!

Places to Visit or Contact
DC Visitor Information Center
1300 Pennsylvania Avenue NW
Washington, DC 20004
202/328-4748
For more information about visiting Washington, D.C.

The Historical Society of Washington, D.C.
801 K Street NW
Washington, DC 20001
202/383-1850
For more information about the history of Washington, D.C.

INDEX

Bye, Capital City.
We had a great time.
We'll come back soon!